IMPURE

UNIVERSITY OF CENTRAL FLORIDA
CONTEMPORARY POETRY SERIES

UNIVERSITY PRESS OF FLORIDA

Gainesville · Tallahassee · Tampa · Boca Raton · Pensacola · Orlando · Miami · Jacksonville

IMPURE

TONY BARNSTONE

04 03 02 01 00 99 P 6 5 4 3 2 1

04 03 02 01 00 99 C 6 5 4 3 2 1

Library of Congress Cataloging-in-Publication Data
Barnstone, Tony.
Impure / Tony Barnstone.
p.cm. — (University of Central Florida contemporary poetry series)
ISBN 0-8130-1689-4 (alk. paper). — ISBN 0-8130-1690-8 (pbk.: alk. paper)
I. Title. II. Series: Contemporary poetry series (Orlando, Fla.)
PS3552.A7215I56   1999
811'.54—dc21   99-14964

The University Press of Florida is the scholarly publishing agency for the State
University System of Florida, comprising Florida A & M University, Florida
Atlantic University, Florida International University, Florida State University,
University of Central Florida, University of Florida, University of North Florida,
University of South Florida, and University of West Florida.

University Press of Florida
15 Northwest 15th Street
Gainesville, FL 32611-2079
http://www.upf.com

for Ayame Fukuda

CONTENTS

LOVE'S MEAT

ACKNOWLEDGMENTS

The listed poems below have appeared in the following journals, anthologies, and prizewinner publications, sometimes in earlier versions.

The Centennial Review, "Surfacing," "Static," and "Descending"; *The Seattle Review,* "Why I Play Video Games"; *The Literary Review,* "The Video Arcade Buddha"; *Agni,* "Hair" (published as "Violence"); *Nimrod,* "Root Hair" (published as "Errand in the Wilderness") and "The Dump"; *Rome Art and Community Center Newsletter,* "Fog" and "Her European Laughter" (published as a single poem); *The Sow's Ear Poetry Review,* "Desire"; *The Berkeley Poetry Review,* "Hair of the Field" (published as "The Field"), "Seen from a Window" (published as "Distance") and "Ars Poetica"; *Lunchbox,* "Why I Play Video Games"; *National Poetry Competition Winners Anthology,* "Ars Poetica," "Seen from a Window"; *Polluted Poems: An Anthology of Poems About the Environment,* "The Dump"; *International Poetry Review,* "Dirt Jesus," "Housecleaning," and "Looking Out of the Second Story Window of IKEA at the Tustin Marketplace Mall."

The translation by Burton Watson on page 25 is from *Cold Mountain: 100 Poems,* copyright 1970, reprinted by permission of Columbia University Press.

I would like to thank my teachers Robert Hass, Robert Pinsky, Thom Gunn, Annie Dillard, David Swanger and Tillie Shaw, and express my appreciation for the generosity of friends and family who have been a community of readers for these poems over the years: Willis Barnstone, Aliki Barnstone, Rodney Jones, Tony Hoagland, Amy Benton, David Benioff Friedman, and especially my wife, Ayame Fukuda, who is behind and within these poems.

HAIR

HAIR

Yesterday, as I pumped cold water
into a bucket

and poured it over myself
to bathe in the courtyard of the Snowlands

Hotel, an old monk, watching
from the porch,

came up to me, grabbed a handful
of my chest hair

and tugged it painfully.
He had never seen such body hair,

I suppose. I reached for one
of his hanging mustachios

and pulled it till he yelped.
In this way we understood each other.

LHASA. JUNE, '85.

HAIR OF THE FIELD

Bitter (Anglo-Saxon *biter*). Original meaning, "biting, cutting,
sharp," but now used only of taste. Also, unpalatable
to the mind. Expressing or betokening intense grief, misery,
or affliction of spirit.

Our front yard bursts with clover and dandelions
and long spears of rye and pampas grass

where frizzled neighborhood cats
stalk beetles and roll on their backs.

We are the shame of our neat buzz-cut street,
but we have no lawnmower,

so today my task is to crop this savannah
with a pair of garden shears.

I give the yard a trim and think of Walt Whitman
growing hair underground, his fingers worming

through the soil, green nails clawing toward light.
Passersby stop and smile at me, ridiculous

with my pathetic clippers, but I adjust my baseball cap,
and I am Walt Whitman, young, strong in a teeshirt,

covered in pollen and sweat,
all rude muscle working through the grass.

At the graveyard up the block the beautiful hair
is shaved close to the graves.

It's nice to think the dead push up
into the world as ragweed and sorrel,

the way Walt's words become grass in the mouth,
his delicious syllables: *the smallest sprout shows*

there is really no death. Truth is, the smallest sprout
shows its silver underbelly as I slice off its legs.

4

As I murder grass, it exhales last puffs
of pollen I cough up like bitter seeds.

I am clipping Whitman's nails and thinking about
the tangle underneath out of which rises

even a simple word, like *bitter*,
thinking what would it be like to follow a word back

into the mouth and swim down the column of air
through the babble of centuries?

I open my eyes in a dank Saxon cottage.
There is the smell of cabbage and whale oil.

I have just bitten into a sour apple,
a taste that bites the mouth, and as I spit

the apple flesh onto the floor I cough out
a new word, *biter.* Bitter, bitter.

It rises from the stomach, and it tastes like acid
and loss. It tastes like grass.

Within a year I use the word to name
the taste of a broken longboat, my girl's red hair

sinking in the frozen lake, my land
overrun by people speaking another tongue.

I am standing in a field. And I dive down
the length of a blade of grass underground.

Here all things take shape, rooted in each other,
so the moon that spilled honey on Whitman's head

will be overhead tonight, and long after
the longboat has become a skeleton

half in sand, and the child a seed
in the lakebottom's mud, I taste the biting taste

of grapefruit, appleseed, and go back
into the house with my hands stained green.

ROOT HAIR

When an American looks at a forest,
he sees lumber.

Ralph Waldo Emerson

His mind buzzing with teeth and calculations,
worries he holds at arm's length like his chainsaw,
the foreman lingers after paying the others.

The stump he sits on doesn't know it's dead:
its root hairs still finger through the mulched
generations of leaves and innocently feed.

He thinks of the rutted path out to the highway,
of a small town nearby, the Train Track Bar and Deli
where he'll order a poorboy and share a pitcher

with Mel, who shares his need to get things straight
at the end of the day with a game of pool—
cool combinations of bank and spin and skill

until the final click sends the eight ball
across the green for the kill. But things have a way
of spinning out of control. Drifting home

on the strip of blacktop, some deejay's chatter
starts his mind up again: the BeeGees, PG&E
by tomorrow or it gets cut off, the thumb

Enrique lost at the mill trying to keep
a board straight. It wheels from this
to that all evening until he crawls between

the covers, embracing not his wife
so much as the darkness behind, a place
where the world trickles off

as the nerve-stars spinning behind his eyes
take root and, feeding from an underground
stream, branch and flower into dream.

THE DUMP

I keep coming back to the root systems
of clearcut redwoods dying underground
like coral reefs in the sad oceans.

Men come in from the city to plant new saplings
in grids—planned forests whose tapered fingers
thread down through rusted beer cans,

the thousand-year monument of a styrofoam cup,
and grip buried barrels the way on the ocean floor
giant sponges bubble from the nuclear containers

like cheese clouds. There must be a better way
to say this, how the hills' bad haircut
makes me think of Bill's poor head

after chemotherapy, his body seeded with cancer.
At first, no one knew the headaches
that reduced this gentle man to shaking rage

came from dark tissue rooted in his brain.
We just saw the surface: evil stepfather.
Later the cancer drained him even of violence.

He gave up his job at Westinghouse
and began to forget. When the toilet became
too great a mystery he shat in the dresser drawer,

pushing the mess out into a nest of white shirts.
He must have known it was wrong—
that nightmare handwriting coiled and black

against the cloth saying *waste, waste.*
Somehow the body's hard potato had turned
dark and soft and he'd drape a clean shirt

over the decay to put a skin between his mind
and that thought—like white sheets in a hospital
screening patients from each other's loss.

When I was a kid we used to swim near the plant
where he worked, diving from limestone towers
into the deep water of the quarries.

That was before what happened in our town surfaced
as lesions on the skin. Now the old men
from the plant who used to wade calf-deep in PCBs

are dying of leukemia, the children still-born, or, like me,
growing up in the scruffy woods, waiting for summer
when we dived off high towers into the cool green

dumping grounds of the old men's poison.
But it's bigger than that, bigger even than the secret
death I think is going on beneath my skin.

If you drive just outside of town
you come to the landfill where labels peel off
but the products remain, patented generations

under a film of earth. At the end of the day
the last, loaded pickup trucks climb to the dump site,
leaking milk cartons, plastic toys, hula hoops,

dusty tire rims, and the man atop the bulldozer
smokes a cigarette as he waits to seal the broken earth.
Beyond the dump the hills are tossed

with red pine; in the empty sky turkey buzzards
hover like tiny hands. This is something
the mind can grasp. But below the earth

these things endure: the migration of chemicals,
rates of mutation, plumes of dioxin spreading
like a drop of ink through a glass of water.

HER EUROPEAN LAUGHTER

These days when I see my mom she sits me down
for a formal talk about where the jewels
are stashed and which bonds she's cashed

and this is the closest we get to talking
about the thing bearing down
on us. "Don't cash these ones"

she says and I notice a fine threadwork of lines
across her beautiful face. "Here's the key"
she says, "behind this box," and I see sunspots

flaring on her small hands.
She drives me to the airport
and all the way to St. Louis I try to remember

what she said, but my sullen mind refuses,
ferociously forgets. I remember
her high, rich voice, her quick, high-heeled steps.

"When I die . . ." she says, but my ears
have already flinched away from hearing.
"You must remember," she says,

and I try to store this tremulous smile,
her European laughter, the taste
of last night's stew

of spinach, rice, and feta cheese.
"Call me when you get there,"
she says at the gate. Powder, perfume, kiss.

The rich trill of her voice calling
after me down the tunnel insists
"Don't forget!" And then she's gone.

FOG

Now in the St. Louis airport, coming home to you,
I sit among the strangers, each within our castle
of boxes and suitcases. The man next to me on the phone

is saying "It seems every time I leave home
on a business trip some tragedy hits,
the dog gets killed, you get in a wreck."

"We can't do this," he says, "we can't do this . . ."

There's enough snow on the intercom
to keep us here a week, but the voice is saying
"fog in San Francisco," and the flight

back to you will be delayed indefinitely.
I wish with distance I could see
how this problem came between us,

everything clear and miniature in the eye
of a telescope, see how to fix it,
but I don't know where to begin,

how to work this thing.
No one reads the fine text
beneath the words I love you,

where our sweet pathetic flesh
is simplified to diagrams and ways
to fit part A with part C,

some parts not included.

"What do you *mean* you won't go?"
the man is almost shouting now,
pounding the words down like nailheads into wood:

"Can't I leave for two days
and make some *money* for our *family*
without you *pulling* this *shit?*"

Somewhere, past the grid of fire that is St. Louis,
along a thousand miles of phone line
planted like nerves beneath the great salt plains

and the wilted white flesh of desert mountains,
his wife with a stabbing headache
and a pain in her ribcage

won't go to the hospital,
doesn't want to know
about X-rays and CAT-scans.

Because there are some things
you can't fix with words or tests
and some things you can't keep in a box.

Some things erode you more
than the minutes, days and months,
so you end up avoiding doctors,

flying blind through a fog of not knowing
like all those stupid galaxies
still flinching away from the original mistake.

In the end it's a woman's voice that says
"Ladies and gentlemen, thank you for your patience,"
and we know the big change has come at last.

It comes with a whisper of escaped air
like a sigh into the phone as the man says
"This is going to be a big mess,

I don't even want to think about it."

DIRT JESUS

Muscled and sleek as an adder,
the dogwood in our backyard
snakes underground with a thousand tiny mouths.

I think of it tentacling
through the earth's mineral mind
like a cancer,

feeding on its own death,
dropped limbs rotting and turning to dirt,
the acid taste of lost leaves,

and it sparks a fear, like the gerbil
who eats his swarming pups
on the altar of the exercise wheel.

Yet it is spring, and eating an apple
on the back porch and dangling my legs,
I am happy shedding my skin, spilling

my breath. The woods are wet,
the black soil steaming, ice sheaths
drop in small damp tinkles

and already the first buds flame
from the dogwood.
I walk into the blossoming and imagine white

hands welcoming me to my death,
a bonfire of lives and leaves
changing form,

as if this were rebirth:
nature tugging at the generous corpse
and blooming with hungry life.

All the gods living in the leaves

of books came from these trees:
Jesus grows toward the light dumbly,

forgetting he is or is not the messiah.
Buddha's damaged flesh is chemical sap.
They tangle underground through skeletons

and mulch, metals and ghosts,
and their mindless ecstasy is all
the redemption there is, and they live.

FOR GERALD STERN

DIFFICULTY

There's something to be said for difficulty,
Michael says as he pours the wine,
and my wife gives me a hard look
I take to mean, look at your napkin,
you barbarian! No one notices, I swear,
as I sneak the white square onto my lap.
They're listening as Michael tells us
how the French plant grapevines
in difficult soil so the roots elongate
through the dour earth, drilling down
until they find deep water that distills
as it branches up the capillaries
and spills into the fruit as essence
balled up in a little green horizon,

and how there's something to be said
for ease, for the California wines, flagrant,
in your face, those lush flavors
dancing with anyone for a few bucks,
fruit popping out of their blouses.
There's something to be said
for the quick fix, though the flavor
becomes vinegar in a few years,
whereas the difficult wine
left untapped in the cellar
quietly burns off the dross,
spirit stepping out of skin
and flesh and turned low like a flame
flickering at the tip of the wick.

When we leave the restaurant
the condensation on the windshield
has pulled into small globes
across which sail tiny moons and stars
and satellites that the wipers scatter

when Michael turns on the engine.
I am thinking of what he said before,
of the way a seed holds the whole plant
inside, and I imagine a planet
in each grape, with green seas, ships nodding,
meditating clouds, islands in clusters,
villages and fortifications budding, farmers
with their goats, dolphins rolling,
wrecks turning beneath the waves,
and the full moon flowing overhead.

Now my wife leans in as if for a kiss,
then gives a sharp nibble to my lower lip.
In her eyes shines the great city.
Our headlights drown in those lights
as Michael maneuvers us through
constricted streets onto the onramp
and jets us across the concrete sky
of the freeway, and I sit in the back
savoring something difficult to love
and even more difficult to uproot,
the taste of wine, the taste of blood.

FOR MICHAEL SCOTT SMITH

LAUNDROMAT

The swirling washers sound a siren call.
Listen long enough and they'll pull you under
with the clothes. The weather's turning bad.
Thunders kick through the darkness outside,

and against one wall a row of video games glints
faint threats of *Primal Rage* and *Mortal Kombat.*
Into the empty coin return a child shoves
two chubby fingers, hits the red plastic button,

then feels again for change inside the metal slot.
He pulls and punches the dead joystick, reaching up
on toetips, but the impassive glass just scrolls
a top-score list up the screen. ZAP, WIZ and KIL were here,

and for ten blocks, phonebooth glass, retaining walls,
and underpasses are scrawled with bright ballooning tags
they hope will not wash out. Loose change in a dryer
rattles like dice in a cup, chatters like dice

about to be thrown. The washers whirr like small tornadoes
spinning houses and tractors and cattle dry, yet
on gentle cycle they soak and murmur *the world's just fine,*
since gravity will keep us from shooting off into space

and the addict waiting between the cars
will be cleansed in the confessional of his dreams.
A worn jangle from the metal bell above the door
and four young mothers look up from the folding counters.

Their nervous attention rises and swivels in unison,
sights the young couple wrestling in the doorway
with four duffels and a baby carriage, then drops back
to the clean, soft folding. No cruiser angling

for a driveby, no crazed ex-husband stands there, no angels
dangle from the streetlights—only the video machines
call like pulsars from across the universe
with soft karate screams and news of solar flares.

Her eyes half closed in pleasure, one mother gazelle
arcs her delicate neck and nuzzles warm laundry
like shoots of young grass. She is innocent as honey.
And the baby clothes smell so sweet and chemical clean

no danger could be inching his belly through the night,
his brain a swarm of stingers and black fur.
The sound of the washers murmurs to you
to drown among blue leaves pressing

against the window, blue leaves shifting,
and the sweet lights flicker and a light hail
spills through the planet's turning darkness,
change in the dryer rattling, loose teeth in a skull.

LOOKING OUT OF THE SECOND STORY WINDOW OF IKEA AT THE TUSTIN MARKETPLACE MALL

it seems a new nature has bloomed
in the fields where fruit groves once hung
sweet bulbs: above the gas station
a lit globe beckons orange as a gumball

and at the mall entrance a neon spray
proffers a turquoise, red and yellow bouquet
to the yellowjackets diving, to red ants
swarming on the rainslick freeway.

Faintly a car alarm wails on and on
like an old London ambulance,
comic in its urgency,
but no one checks to see what's wrong.

I look down to my plate of Swedish meatballs,
to the packages leaning against the table leg,
then out again to murky shiftings
in the starless sky, to the air darkening

like my lungs, like the smog and toxic groundwater
that stains your thoughts, always murmuring
in the background *cancer, cancer*.
I guess you could say it's beautiful,

this valley like dark water
through which weave lit aquarium fish,
darting, many-colored, sleek and carniverous,
parked cars awash with glassy light,

and the way, in one corner of the lower sky,
the full moon glows white as a cut radish,
a light bulb left on
after the people have left the house.

FIRST MEMORY

I waver behind glass, the wool blanket
pulled around me in a blue womb,
and look out at the fields sifting darkness,
birches papered over with silver.

The friendly stable where horses,
sweet-smelling manure and leather
greet me in the mornings
opens like a deep cave

while something cratered white in the black
windowpane rises over the fields.

I am so young that I'm still waking up
from the death before life,

and my shining mind doesn't know
the names for strangeness, moon,
the sleepwalking dream in which I climb
back into my crib and wrap
the soft blue sky around my fear.

And so the question tumbles like a bright coin
through the astigmatism of memory
as I fall through the covers and the years
away from the house on Long Swamp Road
and the horses we had for just that summer.

Even now, when sleep lowers the mind
I swim in tall grass of an undersea field,
I am searching for the horses
but they've gone wild
and slip away in the swelling grass.

There is an architecture to the mind,
unknowable, though rising into dreams.

It could be the lichens that constellate
on shale outcroppings in Mr. Ketchum's pasture,
gray Rosetta stones whose hieroglyphs elude
—and then one day come clear.

It could be a clearing in the woods
I find one day (a secret meadow
where the deer beds lie) and can't find again
though I search the mountain for thirty years.

Or it is this old white house
where a boy watches
from the second story window

as I sway through the field of milkweed
and black-eyed Susan
to the place I was always going.

The dark throat of the stable opens before me.
Soon I will understand.

NO VACANCY

"Jesus Saves—Shouldn't You?"
Bank billboard in Bloomington, Indiana

1.

The 40-watt moon spins like a plastic globe
lit up from inside and plugged into the wall,
and lifts the buoyant mind

of a teenager smoking on the yellow hood
of a '64 Mustang, back against the cool metal.
He floats across the invisible blacktop,

the light punching slats through the thin mist
in windowsquares, up into the watery dark
where blue coils spell out the night's *vacancy*.

This is me, age fourteen, smoking grass
in the parking lot of the *Powwow Motel*.
I see the dead promise of *magic*

fingers in grayed-out neon, and feel ordinary
magic as a deep wind combs fields
and drives into the Indiana woods.

Two dimestore Indians darken the painted *Entrance*,
mahogany-varnished, their hands upraised
in wooden greeting. Like magic they stir

a memory in the dark that flickers
black and white like trees against snowfields,
a rickety projection on some classroom screen

—of a shadowed path, a dry flutter
of leaves, and a Shawnee warrior
taking musket shot in the heart for manifest destiny.

2.

It is a damp night in 1769, and leaning into the fire
men in animal skins cast hairy shadows
while the logs give up the flesh. Flames grasp

at the impassive moon. Skinned rabbits hang from
a low branch, translucent in the milky light.
The men are brothers, almost alone it would seem

in the continental woods, what remains
of seven friends who died blundering
through paradise, the loudest things in the forest.

They have walked here from Pennsylvania,
the creeping edge of the colonies, and are jittery
as locusts. They gaze into the pine air and dark

shocks sprout along their branching thoughts
with each *shift* and *crack* from the surrounding night.
The promised land is awake and watching them.

It is preparing them a surprise, tugging at leaves
to decorate their entropic flesh, to cover
the congealed eyes, the lids peeled back in terror.

3.

The land took them inside, two bad seeds
pushing into the Devil's territory in search of fur
and a place to settle God's People, and now,

above the anonymous mounds in the forest,
at Tippecanoe and Fallen Timbers, the old molecules
of white devils and the Shawnee Prophet

spin through the air like planets released from orbit,
a ghost flight of bullets and arrows prickling
the skin of a boy riding the hood of a yellow Mustang

and then cast off with a shudder.
The dead God planted in the corn fields
and trailer parks sparks to electronic life

along fiberoptic cable lines of Christian TV
and turns the motel windowpanes a holy ghost blue.
Across the parking lot a homeless man

mumbles from his nest of boxes:
I just got out of the hospital, I've had my heart
and lungs removed, I'm going to night school

and trying to get ahead. Endless hope.
Crosses are burning in the woods,
bones break beneath the plow,

the Shawnees are just a lesson to teach
stoned kids in school, but somehow
the world is all before us, spinning

like the moon above the line of trees.
So I light up another joint, and listen
to the blur of late traffic along the interstate

chasing after the dream and the promise
on billboards for banking and Jesus.
It's just ahead, bathed in floodlit glory.

VIRTUAL BUDDHA

My mind is like the autumn moon
Shining clean and clear in the green pool.
No, that's not a good comparison.
Tell me, how shall I explain?

Han Shan (8th–9th century)
Translated by Burton Watson

THE VIDEO ARCADE BUDDHA

The video arcade Buddha looks like any other Buddha,
could have been transported whole from a shrine
in Nepal or Burma: chest sagging above a pot belly,
wooden, painted limbs pretzeled into the lotus position.

The glass eyes watch absently as surfers and deathpunks pass
in a scratched, fingerprinted, plexiglass haze.
The boy with the dangling crucifix and Whitesnake teeshirt,
eyes still glazed from the early show at the Starlight,

wheels off from a flock of heavy metal bighairs
and postures before the machine, trying to figure.
There are no instructions, only a quarter slot.
He's put off, but he puts it in, if only to watch what happens.

A bell rings and with a jerk the hidden clockwork
starts to turn; the right hand lifts from the knee
and gestures mechanically, and the wooden mouth hinges
mutely open and shut. A fortune in a plastic bubble

drops into the shelf below like a slot machine in Reno,
and the wheels spinning the Buddha into animation
suddenly stop. Who knows what fortune he's bought?
Maybe it says "Live long and prosper"

or "Never give a sucker an even break,"
but the bighair walks off looking disgusted,
and, until his next cheap incarnation, the Buddha settles
into nothingness, a panhandler between handouts,

his heart connected to the same wire
as the metal bell, and his eyes empty, empty.

STREET CORNER IN BERKELEY

"Spare change for drugs?"
the homeless man asks,
and something rivers through his narrow frame,
backs up in his throat behind a knob of phlegm
and starts to choke him,
an unseen fist shaking him right out of his skin.

Clot of bearded flesh, his eyes glitter like tin,
watching as he puts out a serious hand
and asks again,
"Spare change for drugs?"
But he can't help it.
The seizure hits and laughter spasms through
his body bunched up like a kiss.

HOUSECLEANING

After cleaning house everything is tamed for a while
but still running down. The entropy of dirt and clutter
is swept and straightened, boxed and folded, the floor waxed,
socks matched. The loveseat and clawfoot dresser,
the stolid arabesques of the rocking chair, dully shine
in the living room. Even the air has thickened and set.

And when it's time to lay myself in bed
I do a last somnambular round of the house,
flicking off lights, emptying the dishrack, and just before
crawling between the sheets, place my finger on the windowpane
that always shakes with wind or heavy traffic.
A second later it rattles again.

Look, here's my body shaking on the bed,
and there a semi trembles through the underpass,
chasing a yellow line unwinding into distance.
I lift like dust and drift toward what
wheels hugely by just past the windowglass.
I can feel the membrane between us.

Give me your hand. It's easy when we dream.
Lights of my neighborhood float by like confetti
and everything quakes with a violence barely restrained,
our hands gripping the great wheel, the effort it takes
just to stay in this body, the engine roar always threatening
to tip the cup from its precarious perch on the dash.

WHAT WE CANNOT KNOW

is always driving past, the mosquito whine of traffic
pricking the mind, but if you give in to the dream
you might wake up behind the driver's eyes, gazing
at your red calloused hand lightly resting on the wheel.

It's better like this, the three of us together in the truck,
three characters exchanging faces in a dream,
each imagining he is the sleeper who made up the world.
Last streetlights stream across the waxed blue hood.

We're going off the edge of town into invisible fields,
past darkened country houses, towards a radio tower
whose cherry beacon punctures the sky
yet always retreats behind the next bend.

It is a question of faith in the road
that makes us drive through the night in sunny denial
like California dreamers, putting the pedal
to the metal, admitting nothing of the tectonic

strains that with a shift could cant the rigid freeway
up beneath our wheels like a drawbridge,
concrete pillars snapping like breadsticks—
It's better to drive on despite the nails

shivering against the metal floor, the rattle of tools
behind the seat, a belt whining in the engine.
Better not to worry about the new crackling
in our joints, and the hairline cracks in snapshots

from our youth, and how with a simple hiccup in the engine,
a piece of gunk caught in the wrong valve,
we could fly right out of our bodies
and drop forever through icy zero

along with the whole dilapidated universe.
It is better not to wake up from the dream,
not to know what is behind the big question mark.
Better to keep driving away from

the question and fling ourselves down this line
of headlights as if the moving were all
that keeps us from falling
out these eyes and down the tunnel of trees.

MAIL SLUT

The Soul selects her own Society—
Then—shuts the Door

Emily Dickinson

She calls him Mail Slut because he waits
by the box, his heart quietly ballooning
for the Chinese postman to hand him
the latest rejections with a smile.

They leave a scar,
these afflictions sent by airmail,
but how much better
than the zero of an empty box

to pull against delicious gravity,
orbiting off to water the bulbs,
to pay the Visa before it crushes him,
while the universe shifts

off center and starts
to fall into the white rectangle
left unopened on the table.
"Hello, Mail Slut," she says at the door,

keys in hand, then leaves him
to enjoy the wild mutilation
of hope. When the envelope
opens him up, the cut goes deep.

He tilts Dickinson down from the shelf,
miserably reads the letter
she wrote to the world, that never
wrote to her. She says publication

is the auction of the mind,
that the brain is wider than the sky,
and sure enough his head swells up
like the planet as words buzz his ears

and occasionally drop in flame
like bits of spinning space junk.
He knows. Junk is junk.
The bulbs are rotting in the ground.

But he collects what falls
out of the air—booster rockets—old space suits,
and like some mad engineer
starts to build again.

"I'm going, Mail Slut," she says,
but he's already left, drifting like a comet
among the cotton stars, in a place where
he can wait by the box, tinker

with the fence, dig around for
his superglue, and listen
in the cosmic silence to the hiss
of his oxygen leaking away.

JOY OF PISSING

He who holds fast to the Way
Desires not to be full.

Lao Tzu

In the restroom
at Berkel Berkel's
Korean sushi restaurant
my body drains—
a whole summer of sunlight
balled up in oranges,
sliced, crushed, stored
in cartons of Tropicana,
and after coursing
a short time through
the consumer, me,
pouring its battery acid
in an acrid stream
from this flesh pipe.
I am in a sleepy haze.
It's good to let go
of what you've taken in.
I don't even look
at the condom machine
with its pleasant promises,
or the hieroglyphic walls,
but gaze mildly
at the pure, unassuming white
of the toilet bowl
that lifts an orange circle
of water in its porcelain arms
as if it were a statue
in some rank and forgotten garden,

slimed green, pissed on
by dogs and transients,
but still raising a bowl
of mossy fruit, a serene
offering to the universe,
in its stone arms.

PISSING OUTDOORS

I'm speaking this poem into a tape recorder
while pissing into the wild Aegean,
my thin arc hitting rock and bursting above
the sea which shoots its jet up to meet mine.
And I wonder what is this great pleasure?
Is it visceral instinct,
red prick squirting a mailbox
from beneath an upraised leg?
Maybe the secret joy
of getting away with something,
sprinkling underwater in a public pool
and the face above beatific
as a medieval madonna.

It's good to free your penis from its cloth.
It spends so much time wrapped up,
restrained, tucked safely away
like relatives shuffled off to rest homes,
the idiot child fed blubbering and sloppy
in a back room by the nurse.
Let it hang out in the wind,
feel the fine hairs of the crotch
stand up and shiver in the breeze.
Let it dangle, angle as it wants, and release.

It's good to have a penis,
even though we keep it safely holstered.
My message today is, treat your genitals well.
They do a lot for you.
Let them air out, let the wind cool them.
Piss in woods among the tall naked trees.
Piss in the sea which sounds watery beneath
and blends in this poem into tape hiss.
Piss on the rocks, acid etched into limestone chalk.
Piss in the field and leave your mark

like deer beds and alien crop circles,
and then after you've clomped and shuffled off
through the brush, loud as a bulldozer,
the animals will reappear,
looking about, delicate ears alert,
and sniff that unfamiliar fragrance,
wondering what new creature has passed their way
and left its scent, lingering.

PURE POETRY

"That's pure Tony," my father laughed
when I showed him my new poem
on the joy of going out into nature

and pissing on it, and I winced
as if the edge of that laugh had sliced
some tender bit of skin,

the same way I said *ouch!* as if gashed,
when a friend wrote me
that my work was "scary"

and "really Midwestern somehow."
Of course, it was in the Midwest
that people walked out of my readings

looking distressed, as if my poems
meant things that poetry is not meant to mean.
Look, if I'm next to you in line for a show

I won't cut ahead. I keep my eyes demurely
averted from the men squirting
next to me into the rusted urinal.

And going home I don't veer from lane
to lane, honking and slamming my hand
against the dash because I want

to slash in front of you on the road.
But at home, alone at night,
it's hard to be polite

as it is to understand how
the deep cut on my finger
knew to harden and dry

and shed itself in a layer of dead skin
until it was just finger again.
Or why the force

that through the veins drives my body
spilled out from the wound
bright and flagrant crimson,

then burned into white
carpet and pants, darkening, impure
stain that won't wash out.

THE BOG

The body is always discharging matter like a ripe boil ... wax from the ears, snot from the nostrils, and from the mouth, food, bile, phlegm, and blood, and from the two lower orifices of the body faeces and urine, while from the ninety-nine thousand pores of the skin an unclean sweat exudes attracting black flies and other insects.

the Visuddi-Magga

I could take a syringe filled with black coffee
and plunge it in my heart
and my brain would still be filled with mud,

like those bogs where the porcelain limbs
of Irish lads float in embryonic peat.
         Meanwhile, I sit here, lost in morning fog

and pushing shit like an unwanted customer out
the door of the body, sucking air through
the nostrils, giving out scent from my pores,

pheromones from my hair, and think how
with every instant I am instantaneously
losing and gaining the world,

a Grand Central Station for molecules and minerals,
viruses and cabbages and turds,
trains coming and leaving at all hours

while the hands of the big central clock
keep whirling around the same hub,
and I test one word against another,

bath or gap, mud or crap, as if the right word
merely whispered could stop
all the hormonal traffic,

trigger some alarm and wake me up.
         Meanwhile, from a million toilets
black torrents spill underground

through the branching tubes
into the mother pipe, eighteen feet around,
and in the treatment plant the workers rake condoms

from the grill, and syringes, even paper bills
flushed as the cops broke in the door,
and pour chlorine into holding tanks

still rolling with tarry life
before the big release into the ocean.
         Meanwhile, the mortician drains blood from a tree

of veins set in the flesh of the dealer who took
a bullet in the eye when the cops broke
in the bathroom. He looked up

into the face of the man who was killing him
and what he saw woke him
out of his body, which has begun to decay

like the new light that keeps blowing across the white
enameled table and bouncing its billion
photons like fleas off the furniture.

         Meanwhile, the bog boys float in dirty soup
through the centuries, mouths locked open
in a last desperate "I am,"

bodies curled into a question mark,
and on my porcelain seat I close my eyes
in the unmentionable joy of shitting the world out

of me, and I'm glad I was made to thrill
at eating and shitting, at breathing, coming,
at all the traffic through the body's doors

that I'm helpless to stop.
It lets me put a good face on all this loss,
like the mortician carefully parting

the dark hair, powdering the face,
and considering the ruined eye
while the embalming pump shudders on the table.

SEEN FROM A WINDOW

Seen from a window high over
the street, the drunk's shirt
is a flag pulled on a blue wind
as the policemen struggle
to rein him in. A car slows down
to watch, an old Chevy, tailfinned,
chromed, all liquid light and wax,
and two faces shine within
before it roars up Twin Peaks
through the calm repetition of stoplights,
an upward smear of taillights
entering into the orange fog
where the city reflects on itself.
From that height San Francisco is
a placid map of mist and light,
stars like clear stones in shallow water,
a high wind breathing past
tranquil as a saffron monk on a mountain.
The monk would say indifference
to misery of the world
is perfect peace, as if it were possible
to trade places with my reflection
in the dark windowglass and watch
myself from the outside, calmly
recording the rise and fall
of nightsticks and my horror,
and as calmly becoming glass again.
So why as the police car swirls out
candy beams of light
am I shouting against the glass
cocksuckers! motherfuckers!
as in a whirl of hair the drunk
goes down at last, and one cop
looks up from the kill
to the lit square of my life
with such certainty, such calm.

MOONSET IN LAGUNA BEACH

Such certainty, such calm in the old stone face
it makes you want to smash it one.
I like to think it random as a flipped coin,

flagrant as a bare ass, teenage with tragic acne,
but the moon doesn't care what I call it.
Broken face of a comparison, it plummets away

from meaning and is not changeable like the sea
—as the sea is not tortured glass. There's no fighting it.
Bash it with a baseball bat and it still won't be

a fly ball dropping white into a prairie of blue grass.
What happens now is nameless, shifting,
continents lost in the sea of traffic behind a line

of trees, a surf punk slipping off the edge of *huh?*,
a dark *what* tangling the fisherman's net.
Cicadas whine, *not like high tension wires*

I admit, and crush one into the sand.
And yet on a cliff overlooking the sea
the pleasing asymmetry of a pine

desiring light, flinging its limbs outward,
is almost a kind of thought.
It has changed into the shape of its need

for light, so that it's possible to imagine the tree
is lightning branching up to meet the sky,
each green needle quivering electric

as the dramatic arms grapple with that
resounding roundness, that bright bulb,
golf ball in the air, that white onion moon.

WHY I PLAY VIDEO GAMES

It's Rock 'n' Roll 'n' Bowl night.
The pins are flying, and machines call
from the arcade like stripjoint hawkers
selling electric bliss—a mantra of jazz riffs,
mad reiterations of Beethoven,
bops and bleeps and crashes
repeating like jawlines, nose bulbs, cheekbones
through the generations of machines.
I seek this cheap cacophony as a ritual of escape,
joining rows of video addicts as serious
in their pursuits as twenty monks at prayer.
And what would you have me do?
Wear a saffron robe and curl around myself
in the park? No, there is something here
at the center of the discord, a kind of exhaustion
that comes when you've found the rhythm
of your machine, a pattern reeling through you
until you can close your eyes and see
mandalas of light form and deform,
reeling and unreeling until you feel
its simple story might almost make you real.
Small, a small heroic endeavor:
I cannot be what I am
so I become money, quarter by quarter,
and live as long as I can live.

MEAT

On the hottest day of the year I do a little dance
not to step on someone's lost glove,
which pushes against the concrete
stubborn as a prizefighter trying to raise
his wobbly sack of flesh up off the mat.
I almost pick it up, like a two dollar bill
or a Susan B. Anthony, but the flesh won't move,
I swear it's coming off like chicken
simmered slow till it drops from the bone.

The sky flares white and I think ice cream,
arctic expeditions, the Nestea plunge, oases in the desert
and bottomless sodas, not bad as paradises go.
I could be a palm tree fingering the stars,
cool as freezer frost, if I weren't sheathed
in the sweat and flush of this flesh.
How cool it would be to pull off these hands,
to check my head and heart at the front desk,
to kick off my legs like pants
just to watch them fly into the gutter
while the universe flames like paper.

How cool to order up a frosty mug cold as death,
and then to exit the bar, delicately stepping over
my amputated feet, the hands reaching out,
and the penis still trying to bury itself in the sky,
ducking my head to avoid meeting
these eyes that roll back in the heat
and gaze in surprise at their own meat.

ANTS ON THE GREAT WALL

When you look carefully at the stain
on the kitchen wall, it resolves to a chunk
of ground beef being hoisted magnificently up

by a band of tiny red ants. You can see
they've fallen once or twice by the kicking legs
crushed into the holy meat, the way slaves

lugging great blocks of history were buried
where they fell in the foundation of that wall
known in China as the world's longest cemetery.

As I watch, the top of the sticky flesh peels slowly out,
tilting bodies into the abyss, then hinges back
and slaps into the drywall, spinning red stars

through space to bounce off the planet like hail.
Termite hills in Africa, geometric gels
of the honeybee, these ants following chemical paths,

the patterned mind that thinks itself a cosmos
and then imagines there is no other,
or breaks the world into fearful symmetry,

humans within the wall, barbarians at the gate.
After the wall is built, the First Emperor orders
the ancient holy texts, histories, manuals of stillness

and compassion burned in a great fire
so all knowledge will start with him.
The bonfire lasts two thousand years

and fires the engines of these battleships
where sailors shade their eyes and squint newborn
as whiteness uncreates a Bikini atoll

and undoes the code inside their flesh.
Cancer, impotence, a wasting sickness.
In order to contain the red threat

their children are born half-formed,
their skinless bodies seared a violent pink,
and the wall snakes through Berlin, dividing East

from West, the waters from the firmament.
From this height it's easy to look down
as if from the top of a ferris wheel on the frantic ants

like puny humans milling through a fairground,
workers scattered in a tower's ruins,
or the mind itself wheeling from this to that

but failing to grasp the meat of the matter.
Let me tell you a story. Once there was in Babylon
a funeral for a great king, and a poet unable to sing

about the dead king, till, lucky night, his eyes caught
the morning star flaring toward the horizon.
He wrote *Lucifer, light-bearer, how art thou fallen,*

son of the morning. And once there was a scholar
who read this song to mean the sky had split,
and the king who became a star became an angel

falling as flame from the heavens into the pit.
The mind that creates also divides
darkened earth from the blazing sky of love,

slave from master, Messiah from Jew.
Once there was a night of shattered glass.
Once there was a soap that didn't clean.

Once there was an oven where a fire burned,
and the human smoke that rose was smoke
from the mind that devises, the mind that plans.

Yet look now how the ants regroup,
grapple the unstable meat, tame it,
and launch it up the wall again.

You have to admire them, little sparks,
little builders, carrying that bloody mass
into the sky. You have to despise them,

red swarming on red with such carnivorous
intelligence. You have to forgive me, since now
with a shiver I flick the ball of ants and flesh

into the trash with the bulb of a kitchen match,
spray the strays with cleanser and wipe them
off the face of the wall with a paper towel.

ARS POETICA

Greg told me once in the hotel bar in Kunming
how sitting on top of a rock
on a clear cold day in Yosemite
his eyes snagged on a black line marked across the sky.
For a breath or two he tried to understand it
as a this or a that but couldn't read
the strange black strip in the scaleless blue
until something came over him.
Wings battered his head, a sharp comb scraped
across his scalp, and something gave a quick,
almost tender, tug at his hair.
He nearly fell from the ledge
and before he could tell just what it was
it spun away again, flattened to a line
against a multitude of lines, the ganglia
of forest below, cliff-face striations,
the river's languid scrawl;
and I've always thought this is the way
the line should leave the page,
with extended claws, a sweet and sudden rage.

I READ A BOOK AND IT SAID DEATH

I read a book and it said death.
Dead, it said, dead the seagulls

dropping from the clocktower
on extended wings, dead the watchman

running his stick along the ribs
of a fence at the dark factory, dead light

squeaking over the horizon to play
for a last red minute on my body

bent on a green bench by the gazebo.
And with each dead chime of six o'clock

I shook like a flower under the large rain.
And with each dead chime of six o'clock

I considered eating something greasy and bad,
quesadillas and mu-shu, backribs and gravy,

and I walked uptown past the theatre
on dead streets through dead time,

and a dead child smiled exactly at me
and the night smelled like orange trees

and I said hello to a perfect dead stranger
gave a buck to a homeless man

and I was happy, I was happy.

BLUE ANGEL

I was flying through the blue when the first shot
tore through my shoulder.
I landed hard, and was shipped back to the studio
wrapped in a garbage bag and packed in dry ice
so I wouldn't spoil.
You broke my white wings
and stuffed them with rags and cotton.
You sliced my feathery hide off
and boiled me in a large pot
filled with water and dish detergent to cut the grease.
You scraped off what was left with a dull knife
until I was clean, so clean that not even an insect
could find a snack. You bleached the bones
and stuck them together with superglue
around a wooden frame, and pulled on the feathered hide
like a shirt. Then you sprayed me with gloss
or a satin coat of clear acrylic.
Later, the art critic came and saw me
mounted in the gallery, my wings glistening blue,
and declaimed, "The angel is associated with peace
and its brood normally consists of two eggs.
A study of numerology, as applied to angels,
will add even more insight for you."
There was a musician in the gallery
who was sampling angel cries in his synthesizer.
The critic observed, "The mournful song of the angel
is an indication of water;
the voice of the angel is the rain song.
Their feathers are used in Native American prayer sticks."
I am drifting through the blue with a message,
my wings extended in simulated flight,
each muscle and tendon arranged
in an esthetically pleasing pose,
and a balsa-wood pole through my belly to keep me upright.

FOR BLANE DE ST. CROIX

BLUE NIGHTMARE

The blue insect lashes against my eyes,
tiny planes crash into my eggs and salsa
like dragonflies nosing into tulips
and I wake up moaning ooh, ooh.
Later in the dream I am pushing through the feathery webbing.
On a table is a sky of one thousand blue doves.
They are saying ooh, ooh,
They watch me with their dumb eyes.
They are fragments of your nightmare.
I am falling through the sky's blue web
saying ooh, ooh, and flapping my paper wings,
I don't think they will hold me up.
Later on there are clowns and vampires.
What are they doing in this dream?
The park is filled with dead students.
They are lined up by the highway,
waiting to cross over to the other side.
There is a battering of wings
and a frantic scrabbling of claws.
The cars crawl by like termites
and the sky swoops down from above,
its blue mouth open and calling ooh, ooh.

LOVE'S MEAT

STATIC BLUE

As the television squabbles lightly, you moan
and throw your knee against my back
where I huddle into the blue spray, insomniac,
trying not to wake you. You've tossed the covers off again

and now your fingers crawl anemically across the sheet,
searching. I turn the TV off and sit for a while
in the dark. At first the screen phosphoresces.
Then the room shrinks to a glowing ball,

sensed, unseen walls, and the idea of an outside
scratching against the mind like the barely audible *ksssss*
of a leaf across the windowpane. The furnace idles
and I feel it when you start curling up

like the grubs in our garden that roll
into a rubbery ball if you poke them with a finger.
I don't know where you are, but something,
the line that links a bathysphere to its ship,

joins us. I touch your shoulder and in your dream
I touch your shoulder. You say *Mmmn?* which means
"Are you here too?" I'd like to be, but instead
I draw a dust face on the blank glass,

my finger tripping crackles of static.
Maybe another hour and I can turn off too,
and then all night we'll change and turn
and find each other in the waves—the way

I kiss your forehead now and pull the covers up
and your sleeping hand lifts weakly to my face
and something goes off inside your dream,
a small shock of *It's me.* And you say *Oh.*

SWIMMING NAKED

Yellow threads spread from my splashings
and my penis dangles, bait for quick fish,
as I stitch the rumpled blue silk.

My clothes on the shore, a dark pile.
I stroke and am stroked,
trying to close a blue wound.

BREASTS

Breasts make me happy.
I don't know what it is.
Something about that lift
of the nipple, the urge
to suckle at the tip.
What is it about breasts, the flesh
beneath your hands, jelly of the water,
a peach skin over waves
—what is it about breasts
that makes me so happy?
I know they're marketed to us,
yes, ok, the adult videos,
the soft porn cable where the surgery victims
pretend bliss and try to move
their inflated chests.
Yes I know, sure, what could be more
a symbol of the woman degraded
into an object—two objects
moving beautifully on her chest?
Still, what I'm saying women of the world
is that I love your breasts.
They are light in the bulbs.
They are fullness of the moon.
They are water your hands grip as you swim.
I love breasts with more pleasure
than lifting a ripe peach to my teeth,
more than pissing outdoors
or swimming naked at night
beneath the moon, reaching from the water
up towards that milk.
Why I love breasts I can't say,
but they're electric.

Hell, they're electricity
surging through the genital switch.
They're what turns me on,
I still don't know why,
but at this moment my wife,
who knows me too well,
walks in biting into a ripe nectarine,
sucking sweet juice from the wound,
and says, *mmmmn, good breast.*

A CALIFORNIA COUPLE

"Beat, beat, whirr, thud"
Ezra Pound, *Canto IV*

She has bags of peaches, yellow, unbruised.
As he comes up behind I look away,
don't say hi as they pass. I can't get used
to the ripe crushed fruit of her face,
and wonder who singed her lip
into a sneer of scar tissue,
who put that red hand on her cheek
and caged her up with Mike,
who's just as fast to slap her in the face
as pat her ass when he goes out.
As they step into the rooming house
I see him pet her head, give it a little shove.

The next morning I jump when something
is thrown against the wall so hard
the ceiling cracks and a wisp of plaster drops.
In my room, next life over,
I am judging the relative weights
of a woman's body and a toaster oven
and wondering if I should call the cops
from the payphone at the Shell station on the corner.
I wonder if she hates me for what I hear.
I grab the paper, fix my breakfast.
Eggs are fat eyes that won't stop watching me.
I stab one with a fork
and watch it bleed into the toast.

SICK

Poetry is a cure of the mind.

Wallace Stevens

At the Starbuck's in the Barnes and Noble
at the Lakeside Mall, I am paging through
the Sunday book review and trying to ignore
the planetary globes inflating

a young mother's chest.
The nipples push through her blouse
as if perpetually surprised
by lust. It's easy to be sick to death

from what we do to our residence on earth:
mini-malls and freeways spreading like toxins,
every meadow sprouting condos.
What strangeness to cut off bits

of ourselves, inject collagen in our lips,
starve and pad the poor, insufficient flesh
until it resembles the tissue
of our shared fantasy.

I am reading an essay by Alfred Kazin,
who snipes, "Poetry has little to say
that requires so intricate a form of thinking as poetry."
I wonder if it's a sickness that sends me

back to the back of the bookstore
past the chlorine and body reek of the bathroom
where they keep their madwomen
and hunchbacks and idiot sons

and the thin, elegant, unread books of poems.
I think it's just a body hunger,
the way a body gets when it's gone too long
untouched, waiting like a bell

to be rung by the tongue.
Look over there, see the silent blond child
slung on his mother's hip,
his head almost touching the bottom

of one of those great zeppelins.
What does it do to your sense of proportion
to suckle at something that large
and that hard? It must make you sick with hunger,

all that strained flesh, as extravagent and useless
as poetry. So much damned loveliness,
and yet where is a poem that can push my buttons
and push into my buttonholes?

I know I'm speaking to you in a poem
though we're not to admit it,
it's supposed to be our secret.
But aren't you a little sick too

of that particular fantasy? Let's be honest
about our sexy failed breasts. About our need
to inflate each thought until it fills a stanza.
What if we dropped the charade

the way a lover drops his pants
and revealed something sweet and ugly,
with coarse hair and planted veins,
a drop of cum beginning to form

and looking nothing like dew on an orchid at dawn?
Would you say it makes you sick,
the earth and wetness of that split mushroom
always pointing like a compass

toward the magnetic center of your need?
Do you think no one has noticed
you looking through the books,
your nipples standing at rapt attention?

CRUELTY

The youth group was not really
about religion in those days—
not the holy ghost but the Grateful Dead,

not the wine and wafer
but the joint and kegger,
soft drugs to soften the mind

and on a good Sunday
hopeful gropings
through the hormonal darkness.

Each cell of the tentative hand
would spark and fume in perceptual
confusion as it closed around

a breast or knobby shoulder
—impossible to tell which
through the winter sweaters.

But usually the breasts
were kept hidden away
like holy mysteries

from the hungry masses.
We were mainly hungry for
Cordelia—an import

from San Francisco,
the braless fertility figure
of the under-fourteen crowd.

She wielded her breasts
like the courtesans of old
wielded their fans,

jumping rope in the rec room
and distributing crushing, sexless hugs
that kept us like unwilling monks

in a constant frenzy
of eager and ineffectual desire.
Caught between the doctrine of free love

and the injunction against the sin
of male courtship behavior,
we dreamed of soft scenarios

that were not so different, in the end,
than the Penthouse fantasies
of certain medieval Italian painters

in which the Virgin Mary's
snowy ice cream cone
topped with a cherry nipple

is presented to the mouth
of the baby Rabbi Jesus,
who reaches for the holy milk

with one chubby, pigment-deficient
deracinated hand. But really,
it's not like that at all

outside in the desperate Midwest.
It's something else that rises
raw and cancerous as gasoline

in the druidical farmers
and mechanics as they dance
around the burning crosses

off Highway 37, that watches
through the truncated hedges
and drags blue bodies

into the cornfields,
something pagan and fearful
as need. Inside the church

the innocents sacrifice
their dendrites and neurons
on an altar of LSD

and dream of an economy
of love, not of power,
and we dream that way

forever, while a soft
skin of snow begins to coat
the Indiana hills through the dark

plate glass windows
and with sublime and ritual cruelty
the earth goddess leaps

through the rope again
and again while we watch
in a kind of prayer.

SMOKE AND MIRRORS

It was a kind of teenage prayer, kneeling on the floor
while Nathan placed the paper tab on my tongue,
and a kind of ecstasy, later, when from across the room
came rolling a small moon of shifting script

like a ball of brightly struggling ants.
I've always thought it a globe of language flashing
bright codes from the lizard core of the brain.
Written in chemical strands, seared in seratonin,

the vision never quite went away,
just glimmered forgotten like a mirror ball
hanging from the dark rafters of a high school gym
long after the hipsters burst from their cocoons

of hair and ideals and winged off as lawyers and bums.
Even today I can feel it rotating slowly just inside
my forehead as I look at the menu at Tortilla Flats,
wavering between huevos and a country old-fashioned,

and the price list shudders and flares.
Somewhere between the chips and the salsa
perception shifts an inch and the world begins to slide.
I look around the restaurant's dark interior,

at each isolate booth, where heads dip into tax files
and float like deep-sea fish under liquid globes of light.
Now I am staring at the velvet rose on my table,
and the red layers are radiant, segmented,

and inflating like a balloon full of universe,
studded and spinning with stars and planets.
There is a spark hiding between
the brain's divided loaves, whispering nonsense.

I could bang my head against the table again
and again but I don't think it would shake out.

It's in me now, a riddle, a flame. It is the wind
that the mouth shapes into words. It is the slender

fire that runs through my holy genitals,
though I try not to look as the waitress bends
to pour the coffee, her floral print dress falling
open, and the shivering white globe

of her left breast electrifying my brain.
Better not to look at a language that pure.
Just drink the coffee and let the world
return to its normal buzz, buzz.

Just settle down and watch the biplane lazing
in the plate glass window, skywriting
in fat loops, and try to read the smoke
tearing and shifting in the high wind.

SURFACING

As wind shifts maple leaves
in the window, the luminary clocktower
washes in and out of light,
and seems at last to short out altogether.
Now air is everywhere, blue air
pressing the window, lightly
as sheets against our skin;
we swim in it, so deep our bodies move
like sunken hulls, slow, insensate,
turned on a deep current.
There is a washing together, of traffic,
objects blended darkly on the dresser,
a clock somewhere saying not yet, not yet,
clicking surely toward an alarm;
now there are voices, tiny laughter
from another room, and we try
to be quiet; but the sheets slip from us
and we hold each other, gasping
as we rise toward that clear pane
where the world cries out, no longer
the ocean, but you and me, coming to
the surface, which starts here.

DESCENDING

The smallest ticking of a clock. A soft-
ness we relax into like easing in
a bath, rainwater in the earth. A cough
of engines, then (barely a ringing in
the ear) a car's whining begins to fade
down the highway, a long tunnel of sound.
The town shuts down beyond the windowshade
as we slip through the sheets into the ground
and flow with buried streams. I don't sense you
at the horizon of my body now,
don't even dream as I descend into
a place I cannot name, or tell you how.
The self takes fractions of itself and then
forgets. I'm nothing till I am again.

DANCE, WITH MONKEYS

It is one of the oddities
of our love that if I come out
of the bedroom and see you sitting
in the armchair in a glaze of morning light,
pulling yourself out of sleep as if
from a swimming pool of rubber cement,
even though I know I should wait at least
until your first cup of coffee,
I may shuck down my pants and wave
my Mediterranean ass,
and if I bounce out of the shower
stark naked, scattering gems
of chlorinated dew across the carpet
as I bound from room to room
chirping *ee! ee! ee!*
like some deranged monkey,
you are likely, and in truth this is
why I love you, to strip
off your slip, embrace my wet
and pallid flesh and whirl me
round the living room, round
and around, while from the animal
hunkered at the base
of your spinal column rises
that morning song: *ee! ee! ee!*

ARITHMETIC

How much do you love me, you tease
and I know well enough to recount
the way you ask me to rub slippery sticky
aloe gel on your shoulders
and down your collar bone,
how I feel between my palms
the slender bones divided by flesh,
the addition of skin and scent,
memory and oblivion and sex.
Two eyes, one nose, one mouth,
what could be more perfect?
Maybe the fraction of a smile you give me
secretly across the dinner table
that no one at the party but me can divine,
and later in the loft beneath the mosquito net
the way we take the root of self,
adding one body to another, multiplying
sensation—this arithmetic
we do over and again
as the years subtract themselves
and yet strangely add up to how
many, and how much, and much more.

DAYS OF 1961

I am alone in here, in her,
curled up listening to the double pulse,
but sometimes through the skin
of the universe I hear the sonar echo
of some other place.

The idea of it is planted in me,
a little bean, blind, white and round.

I dream it up
then climb the vine
out of the sky and through a hole in the floor
of a house where the giants eat
and planets crunch between their teeth
like poppyseeds.

Through the window are two hills
with towers
white as corpuscles.
Hospital white, straitjacket white,
two breasts for me to suck.

Beyond that boys run
through the jungle throwing pineapples
and painting each other on fire.

And underneath the ground
planted in black silos,
the fierce cocks wait for the pressure to grow.

They will be released
like teenagers with hammers
to blow a hole in the world.

I am alone in here
mumbling to myself
fee fi fo fum.

I can feel it ahead,
that white violence,
and begin to uncoil.
I shoulder the walls until they burst.
The world is broken.
I push my blind head through its ruins.

DAYS OF 1988

My crazy roommate slams doors.

When she sees me over eggs
in the breakfast nook, she smiles
and neutron bombs go off inside her eyes.

She spins a fierce orbit
from her room to bathroom,
beating time with her clogs
on the wooden floor.

Let all the world know how loud
her anger is.

She leaves her room with pretty paper
posters of cats and ribbons

and slams the door.

She plays the corridor like a drum
(with each sharp step
she is crushing our little heads underfoot)

then slams the bathroom door.

In our student bathroom there is no fan,
so oil paint peels from soggy drywall
and the ceiling blossoms with black mold.

Each night she sits there for hours
naked in the white tub
and she is perfect,
milking the anger out of her long pale limbs.

Her breasts pink-nippled, catholic and upright,
bob like buoys in the steam.

I've learned to piss at J.B.'s Big Boy
across the street.

Better not to knock, better say nothing
or else she'll pull the knob so hard
the whole house will whimper

and I'll hear her horsehooves clap clap home.
Then silence, silence,

and slipped under my door in the morning
a sheet from a pink kitten notepad
scrawled in a childish hand:

"*Please* don't bother me
while I'm in my bath!"

signed with a happy face,
the i's dotted with hearts.

COMMANDMENTS

You shall visit a friend for dinner,
an amazing spread of food and drugs,
and you shall eat too much and you shall
smoke some dope, though it kills the memory,
and as your soul rises on a small metal rocket,
propelled by nitrous oxide into an airless seizure,
shuddering through something better than orgasm,
you shall imagine brain cells popping,
and you shall not care,
and when your friend's lover bends to pour
the wine, a little sloppy, flushed breasts
dropping from her open blouse, you shall not
look away, and when she catches your eyes
locked onto the brown gaze of her nipples
and smiles exhilarated with wine
and desire to see the bottle and glasses
and everything else in the fragile world
shatter and burn, you shall not be able
to keep from smiling back,
and you will drink too much, and you will fall
into the wineglass and into bed,
and you will taste grapes on her tongue,
salt on her thigh, breath in her breath,
and in the morning you will feel like hell
and you shall look in the mirror
at the vein flushing blue and rivering through
the puffed flesh beneath your eye,
and you will roll a dream of apples under your tongue
like a seed, how sweet the cut flesh,
the bulbs swelling red and yellow,
and you will worship her pomegranate lips,
her breasts like gazelles, her golden calves,
and you will tell yourself it is just two sacks
of bones and skin rubbing together like metal and flint,

and later you will call her, feeling helpless,
such is modern life, no white dove or rainbows,
no burning bush,
no mountaintop piercing the water,
just a voice from inside commanding you.

THE GLASS MAN

Unshaven at midnight, I am made
sullenly aware of my body's slight reek
by the nonodiferous distance of the man
who looks out from behind glass,

dumb, detached and mysterious.
Aging cheerleaders dream of cracking
open his diamond heart.

I see him rub his belly,
as if he feels this fierce
simmer at the top of his stomach.

Faker! Why does he act
as though with each breath
glass is breaking beneath his skin?

I was always the fragile one.

Look at him now, pretending to read me
but getting distracted by his own glossy face.

Doesn't he even wonder
what happened on the other side?

Or why the woman, who used to look
so beautiful with her hair gone wild,
smiled at him around
the purple toothbrush stem,

then walked out of the frame
as if she'd simply forgotten
something in the next room?

NICE WORLD

We were a little too high, walking through town,
under a sky so ocean deep and blue I was moved
to say, *Nice sky today,* and a dog all fanged smiles
and hairy muscle bounced by after a frisbee
and you said, *Nice dog.* The grass was greener
than grass, just dripping greenness,
and you took my hand and swung me out
onto a lawn to dance, our feet getting wet.

We walked down to the boardwalk and paid
our tickets for the rollercoaster
and whooped while the whole wooden structure
jiggled and jolted as if about to fall
apart; we dove into the tunnel, surfaced into sun,
climbed clack tick clack to the top
and rolled down again, and you said afterwards

Wasn't that nice? And we stood for a long time
watching a spider make its intricate weave,
and even that was nice, as though
the spider's only plan were to throw a thin web
into the air to catch the light, or something light,
ephemeral, and complicated as beauty.

After dinner I washed the dishes,
water hissing from the tap in a clear braid
that would never run out, and that too
was beautiful, as if there were a god
in the faucet, bleeding clarity for us to drink
and be clean, as if a god were in the grass,
a god in the sky, a god in our bodies in dark
intersection in the student bed,
and a god cried out from our lips
too loud not to wake the housemate
curled into a pillow beyond the thin wall.

You were in me like oxygen in the heart,
and the god blossomed from us
on a stalk of air, and the god left
our lips in small yelps, pants and curses,
and left and left as if the leaving
would never stop until at last today
you said *I don't love you anymore,*
and something drained out of the world,
some fizz or subatomic crackle, and we,
dumb cluster of molecules bumbling apart,
sputtered out like dead seeds,
cut loose like so much loose electricity.

And just like that, everything, the grass
hissing with photosynthesis, the blue in the sky
like me in you, the dog sizzling with joy
at the simplicity of a frisbee in its teeth
and a master waiting to throw it again,
everything now seemed dead,
just a tick clack tick of atom against atom,
pool balls rolling through assigned motions
until they drop into a hole, matter passing
energy into other matter, like nothing mattered,
the sky turning white, the two of us clicking
higher and higher, anticipating the drop will be
the most exciting thing in the world.

CONCUSSION

I was on my knees, holding my head.
I didn't know what hit me,
but it knocked me into the black
like your left nipple pushing through
the light blouse and slamming
through my gray matter
thirteen years ago.
I was holding my head,
trying to keep myself inside myself.
You screamed and ran to get some ice
but I was already out of my skull.
Since then I've been hit by nausea,
exhaustion, veins of fire along my spine,
and every now and then
when you walk into the room
I feel reverberations in my head
like a bell struck again and again
by moonlight, flesh, and hail.

DESIRE

A lizard visits me each night,
squat against my windowpane, snake-headed,
with Buddha's eyes, frail legs hold the fruit
of its body to the glass.

In China the dragons are so huge
their spines are spiked mountain ranges
armored with pine trees,
whole villages spilling light

are their lamplit eyes, and they breathe
typhoons, lick lightning with their tongues.
But your gray body, smaller than my little finger,
curls against the square page

of windowlight like a question mark.
It makes me think how on rare nights
when I was young, a great luna moth, wings larger
than my father's hand, came from somewhere

deep in the woods like a dream emerging
from a darkened mind, and tapped against my window.
It was almost human in appearance, a gentleman
in white tails pirouetting on the stoop

as he waits to be let into the dance.
I felt favored my house was chosen
by this bright creature and slipped the window open
to let it flicker into my living room.

I watched it blunder in white confusion against walls
of bright sheetrock, then try to enfold
the lamps' burning globes in its flammable wings
like a moralist's figure for the dangers of lust.

I had to catch it fluttering in a box, like a heart,
and rush it onto the porch, into the woods,

before it beat itself to death against the cardboard.
Sometimes you need to be let inside

even if it kills you, risking AIDS
or screaming outside your lover's house
till you're taken away. Tonight, though, I'm happy
simply for the company of this nonentity

among dragons, grasping at the light in tiny desire,
the *skkrrch, skkrrch* of miniature claws
scrabbling against the glass that holds it back
from the world inverted in its alien gaze.

FOR TONY HOAGLAND

NOTES

"Root Hair"
PG&E is an acronym for Pacific Gas and Electric Company.

"The Dump"
So far, eleven Westinghouse workers who were exposed to PCBs in my hometown of Bloomington, Indiana, have died of brain cancer.

"No Vacancy"
The Shawnee Prophet was the brother of Tecumseh, a self-proclaimed prophet bearing a message from the master of life directing his people to renounce white ways of life and to return to Native American customs and beliefs. In 1811 he led the Shawnee forces against those of General William Henry Harrison in the Battle of Tippecanoe.

"The Video Arcade Buddha"
"His heart connected to the same wire as the metal bell" is adapted from Hawthorne's *The House of the Seven Gables*. The aristocratic but impoverished Miss Hepzibah Pyncheon is forced to open a shop, despite believing that "a lady's hand soils itself irremediably by doing aught for bread." Soon, however, her hopes become intertwined with the commercial enterprise: "...at this instant, the shop-bell, right over her head, tinkled as if it were bewitched. The old gentlewoman's heart seemed to be attached to the same steel spring, for it went through a series of sharp jerks, in unison with the sound."

"Why I Play Video Games"
Video games come in "generations," rather like movie sequels. Each generation builds on the programming and characteristic style and sound effects of the progenitor, making them recognizable and more easily mastered by those who knew the original.

"Ants on the Great Wall"
The Great Wall was built by the warlike Chin Emperor who unified China for the first time. Known as the First Emperor, he also ordered a great burning of the books of the Confucian tradition.

The death of the king of Babylon is compared in Isaiah 14:12 to the descent of Venus, known as Lucifer ("light-bearer"). A now-discredited interpretation of later scholars was that this passage referred to Satan, and that Lucifer was Satan's name in Heaven before his fall. Such typological readings of the Old Testament were instrumental in the conversion of Satan from a minor devil to the great antagonist of the Christian tradition, and probably resulted from an attempt to adapt aspects of Zoroastrian light-dark, good-evil oppositional theology into the form of Judaism that became Christianity.

"Ars Poetica"
Kunming is a city in the South of China.
"Greg" is Greg Thomas, a professor of environmental law, who told me this story.

"Blue Angel" and "Blue Nightmare"
These poems were written to accompany sculptor Blane de St. Croix's installation *Mourning Doves* at the Art Park in Hollywood, California, and were read at the opening with the electronic accompaniment of Bob Dale. The installation consisted of several hundred gray-blue sculpted doves arranged in clusters in the open-air site.

"Nice World"
See C. P. Cavafy's poem "The God Abandons Antony" and Gerald Stern's poem "Nice Mountain."

UNIVERSITY OF CENTRAL FLORIDA
CONTEMPORARY POETRY SERIES

Mary Adams, *Epistles from the Planet Photosynthesis*
Diane Averill, *Branches Doubled Over with Fruit*
Tony Barnstone, *Impure*
Jennifer Bates, *The First Night Out of Eden*
George Bogin, *In a Surf of Strangers*
Van K. Brock, *The Hard Essential Landscape*
Jean Burden, *Taking Light from Each Other*
Lynn Butler, *Planting the Voice*
Cathleen Calbert, *Lessons in Space*
Daryl Ngee Chinn, *Soft Parts of the Back*
Robert Cooperman, *In the Household of Percy Bysshe Shelley*
Rebecca McClanahan Devet, *Mother Tongue*
Rebecca McClanahan Devet, *Mrs. Houdini*
Gerald Duff, *Calling Collect*
Malcolm Glass, *Bone Love*
Barbara L. Greenberg, *The Never-Not Sonnets*
Susan Hartman, *Dumb Show*
Lola Haskins, *Forty-four Ambitions for the Piano*
Lola Haskins, *Planting the Children*
William Hathaway, *Churlsgrace*
William Hathaway, *Looking into the Heart of Light*
Michael Hettich, *A Small Boat*
Ted Hirschfield, *Middle Mississippians: Encounters with the Prehistoric
   Amerindians*
Roald Hoffmann, *Gaps and Verges*
Roald Hoffmann, *The Metamict State*
Greg Johnson, *Aid and Comfort*
Markham Johnson, *Collecting the Light*
Hannah Kahn, *Time, Wait*
Michael McFee, *Plain Air*
Richard Michelson, *Tap Dancing for the Relatives*
Judith Minty, *Dancing the Fault*
David Posner, *The Sandpipers*
Nicholas Rinaldi, *We Have Lost Our Fathers*
CarolAnn Russell, *The Red Envelope*
Penelope Schott, *Penelope: the Half-Scalped Woman*
Robert Siegel, *In a Pig's Eye*
Edmund Skellings, *Face Value*
Edmund Skellings, *Heart Attacks*
Floyd Skloot, *Music Appreciation*

Ron Smith, *Running Again in Hollywood Cemetery*
Susan Snively, *The Undertow*
Katherine Soniat, *Cracking Eggs*
Don Stap, *Letter at the End of Winter*
Rawdon Tomlinson, *Deep Red*
Irene Willis, *They Tell Me You Danced*
Robley Wilson, *Everything Paid For*
John Woods, *Black Marigolds*

Tony Barnstone is assistant professor of creative writing and English at Whittier College. He has published poetry, fiction, essays, and translations in dozens of American journals. His books include *Laughing Lost in the Mountains: Poems of Wang Wei* translated with Willis Barnstone and Xu Haixin (1991), *Out of the Howling Storm: The New Chinese Poetry* (1993), *The Art of Writing: Teachings of the Chinese Masters,* edited and translated with Chou Ping (1996), and *Literatures of Asia, Africa and Latin America,* edited with Willis Barnstone (1998). Born in Middletown, Connecticut, and raised in Bloomington, Indiana, Barnstone lived for years in Greece, Spain, Kenya, and China before receiving his Ph.D. at the University of California, Berkeley.